LOST HEART?

A Guide To Living From Your Heart In A Broken World

Lost Heart? A Guide to Living from Your Heart in a Broken World
By Pat Stark and Nicole Welch
Published by Covenant Publishing House
26 Lake Wire Drive
P.O. Box 524
Lakeland, FL 33802-0524
www.covenantpublishinghouse.com

Editing by Lawrence Hughes

Cover art by Kjpargeter/Freepik

Printed in the United States of America

ISBN-13: 978-0-578-43227-4
ISBN-10: 0-578-43227-7

Some names and details of the story have been changed, and any similarity between the names and stories of individuals described in this book to individuals known to readers is purely coincidental.

All Scriptures, unless otherwise indicated, are taken from the Holy Bible, New International Version, 1973, 1978, 1984, by International Bible Society.

CONTENTS

INTRODUCTION

LOOKING FOR LIFE IN ALL THE WRONG PLACES

It has been said that out of the heart flow the issues of life (Proverbs 4:23). Far too many have never become acquainted with their own hearts and have lived out of a false self without even realizing it. How do you steward your own heart? What does that even mean?

Let's face it, our world is in pain. Personal pain. Cultural pain. Global pain. Some of us are eating ourselves to death in order to stuff the pain. Some of us are drinking it away. Some of us are numbing out to on a Netflix binge, spending hours playing video games, sleeping with someone we don't really care about, using pornography to create a false life, working to death so we feel validated, or any other myriad of ways that allows us to escape just so we can live the "appropriate" life the world says we should live.

Somewhere along the way we have lost heart. We have lost the fullness of the life that Jesus came to restore. *"Hope deferred makes the heart sick, but a longing fulfilled is a tree of life"* (Proverbs 13:12).

TRUE LIVING

This workbook is about moving from the outer life to the inner life. True life flows from within us, and if we do not progress to this, we will always be without!

In the first chapter of Dan Stone's book called *The Rest Of The Gospel*, he spoke about Christianity being like an old iron bed. It is firm at both ends and sagging in the middle. On one end, you trust Jesus as your Savior and you are forgiven, and on the other end, one day you will go to heaven. In between, he says "it gets pretty desperate, you have lots of questions that all boil down to one: "Where is the life?"

Yes Jesus promised this life, but he also said that "*The gate is small and the way is narrow that leads to life*" (Matthew 7:13). He knew this life was freeing, full of joy and hope and that there is a gate that leads to life. It is real; it actually exists, but it is not so easy to find because apparently only a few do.

Sometimes this gate is not big enough for both ourselves and the "clothes" or "baggage" we carry through life. There is a process, a progression. At first, we are a completely external Christian. This means we find life through other people and material things. Our goal is to get through the gate, and become an internal Christian, drawing our life from Him who lives inside of us. This does not automatically happen when we first get saved.

I know for me, the outer life got exhausting and it wasn't "working" anymore. I knew I was a sinner and forgiven. I knew God loved me and had some blessings for me. I also knew this life was about Him inside of me, but I was not sure what that looked like or how to get there.

For a while, the external life is fun, exciting, just like when you first fall in love...but then it becomes routine, mundane, and we have to keep up the performance in order that we keep measuring up. That can leave us weary!

Christianity begins with us believing that salvation comes as a gift of God's grace and our acceptance of Jesus. However, subtly, it seems that we are left on our own to figure out how to **actually** live by God's power in us. Unfortunately, what begins with God's Spirit, ends up in striving and exhaustion.

"After beginning by means of the Spirit, are you now trying to finish by means of the flesh?" (Galatians 3:3 NIV).

This guide is about learning how to live your own life true to your heart.

Throughout this guide many questions will arise for you to answer. Here are a few to start with:

- When you read about the heart, and it's importance to your life, what is your honest, gut level reaction?
- How do you picture your life playing out?
- How do you view God if you were to be completely honest with yourself?

Many times our view of God corresponds with how we have experienced one or both of our parents.

Example: My father was not trustworthy and as a result, I lived with fear and insecurity, always waiting for the other shoe to drop. Without being aware, I simply transferred that mistrust onto God. That caused me to always need to feel in control because I didn't really trust God to take care of what mattered to me.

We encourage you to do these exercises because in so doing, you will begin to get to know the real you!

You can't bring yourself authentically to someone else without first knowing your own inner self.

"Behold, You desire truth in the innermost being, And in the hidden part you will make me know wisdom" (Psalms 51:6 NASB).

<u>WHAT DO YOU DO WHEN THINGS DO NOT GO AS PLANNED?</u>

God often uses the disruption of our plans to reveal the things that hinder our freedom.

When disruption happens, do you:

- Feel anxious?
- Get angry?
- Blame others, circumstances, God, or even shame yourself with contempt?

- Do you quickly try to fix it? Why?
- What do you believe about yourself if you can't?

There is an often unspoken lie that tells Christians, "You need to figure this life out and make it happen!" We are sold the "American Dream" with the white picket fence and then we spend a lifetime of striving to reach those goals in order to find our own particular brand of happiness.

We "grab" for ourselves like orphans who have not eaten in days because we do not deeply believe there will be "food" enough for the next meal. All too often a panic erupts within us that says we need security and we're supposed to know how to get it. But we don't know, and we wonder, where is God when we need him?

Jesus said, "Do not worry about tomorrow, tomorrow will take care of itself," and we do believe that somewhat in our heads, however our hearts still get trapped in anxiety when our plans get disrupted. Because of the lie we believe, even without realizing it, we can get wrapped up in grabbing and building for ourselves an identity of success to prove ourselves worthy of value and acceptance in our own and others' eyes. God is trying to sever us from the fear of an orphan spirit that creates the need to prove ourselves by gathering external things to make us feel safe. Without realizing it, we embrace a false sense of security.

Our sense of false security quickly vanishes when circumstances such as an illness, a downturn in the economy, the loss of a job, a relationship with any key person begins to unravel or even a hurricane or other natural disaster threatens to destroy us.

When that happens, how do we find peace?

When there is an absence of experiencing the Father's love on a deep level in our hearts, anxiety, fear and striving rule us. Feeling that secure and caring love brings us real peace in the midst of adversity and releases true life within us.

The purpose of this guide is to bring peace and freedom to the deepest places within you. Honestly answering the questions laid out in this guide will help you discover your true heart along with inner peace and freedom.

Real life comes from the inside where the Spirit of Jesus lives, loving, accepting, and completing us. When we are unable to live from there, it simply means there is a blockage and disconnect within us that still needs healing.

John 7:38 reminds us that true life with a release of *"rivers of living water"* is meant to flow from within our innermost being (from our hearts).

If we are honest with ourselves, we are all still searching, quietly desperate, and looking for that life. Most of our activities are still involving the outer life. As Christians, we understand really well the fact `that Christ is *for* me, some of us even get the fact that Christ is *with* me, but few understand the *Christ in me* part. **When he is released in me something good flows out of me.**

Jesus desires to join with you in living your life the way you were originally designed.

A huge problem is that we don't fully know ourselves and have only discovered random bits and pieces of our true selves. We can be like that puzzle with too many lost pieces to really make sense of the finished creation.

As a result, we begin to experience shame, frustration, and just remain lost, or try the opposite to get acceptance, value, and security by over-achieving. Sometimes we give up entirely and learn to simply exist.

PART ONE
DEFINING THE PROBLEM: THE LOST HEART

Where is your heart?

The map at any mall will tell you that "YOU ARE HERE" as a reference point to remind us where we are physically in such a large place. It helps us find our way around.

Just like the map, God is asking man to locate his own heart position. He asks Adam in Genesis "Where are you?" As in any journey, before we can get to where we want to go, we must first identify where we are. When setting out on a trip and programming our GPS, we must first begin with knowing our present location if we want to get to our ultimate destination. However as with any journey, there are usually many twists and turns in between and it's rarely a straight line from point A to point B.

Many people feel fairly confident on their journey and don't even realize they have lost their heart and their way or even where they presently are on the journey. They are living on autopilot as if they are under anesthesia, which deadens a person to any real connection with themselves, God, or others.

One extremely intelligent man I met with would tell me all kinds of facts about his life and how his problems were to be solved Biblically. However he was unable to actually live what he believed and there were all kinds of problems playing out in his family dynamics. I let him talk for a while, and then offered him a different way of seeing the problem. I shared about the hurts of his heart, unhealed wounds that began many years ago and caused his heart to actually shut down. We began to talk about the reality that a deep relationship is meant to share and connect on the heart level, not just with our minds. That is the emotional intimacy we are made for. He began to weep and responded that he had been looking for that his whole life.

We develop the part of us that is easiest to develop, while sometimes abandoning other important parts of our being. As the man in the example above, many people use their intellects as their source of validation and achievement. They live solely out of the wonderful minds God gave them, but falsely believe it is their only way to achieve success.

For others it might be their bodies. Some women continually try to find their identity in their beauty, and some men in their physique, their appearance, being macho.

Many Christians, like I did for far too many years, became 'super spiritual' because it was easy for me and was often applauded by the church.

We are meant to be whole people living from the center of our beings with our spirits, our souls (mind, will, and emotions), and our bodies flowing together in harmony connected to God's Spirit within us. In Matthew, Jesus speaks about all the parts of us flowing together: *"Love the Lord your God with all your heart and with all your soul and with all your mind"* (Matthew 22:37 NIV).

ASK: (referring to heart, soul, body and mind)

- What area of myself have I overdeveloped to the exclusion of other areas? Why?

- When you read the above, what is your honest reaction? Hope, anger, shut down, hopelessness?

THE GREAT DISCONNECT

Just like with our physical heart, if we were to have a blockage or a clot, our life flow would be restricted and we wouldn't function well. My husband was an example of this when he had an undiscovered blockage in his physical heart. Simple everyday living became more and more difficult until he had breathing issues just from walking to the end of the driveway. In the same way when we have an emotional blockage, we might still be existing, while desperately trying to get our life support from outside of ourselves. Instead, our lives are meant to come from within where Jesus dwells.

It's similar to a person with dangerously low oxygen levels in their blood having to carry an oxygen tank with them just to function—that's not how they were designed to live, but it still gives them a semblance of life. Many of us have lived that way. However, since there is no true, sustaining source of life outside of us, we will likely eventually experience burn out, exhaustion, depression, or a generally vague disappointment with life itself.

Unhealed wounds cause us to develop false heart beliefs or lies within.

A heart belief is how we truly feel and believe despite what we know (facts or data) to be true in our mind and thoughts.

Isaiah 28:15b says *"For we have made a lie our refuge and falsehood our hiding place."*

"Make a tree good and its fruit will be good, or make a tree bad and its fruit will be bad, for a tree is recognized by its fruit. You brood of vipers, how can you who are evil say anything good? For the mouth speaks what the heart is full of. A good man brings good things out of the good stored up in him, and an evil man brings evil things out of the evil stored up in him" (*Matthew 12:33-35 NIV*).

Many Christians coming from a place of 'super spirituality' will use the Bible as a band-aid to cover their anxiety about their situation. Years ago, while going through a very difficult season, and still very disconnected from my own heart and emotions, I felt God saying to me, "Stop reading your Bible for you know too much intellectually, but you really know nothing much on the level of your heart." I had been like the Bible answer person for many at that time, getting a false sense of importance through my knowledge.

God asked me not to read the Bible for a very long time because I had to learn those truths in my deepest being. I had to learn to "eat" them, to test them out. I had to face my deepest fears first, and then verse by verse, the words on the page became life to my heart. Very, very slowly I began to walk in them as God brought each verse back to me from memory at his pace, not mine. There would be times I would be in a single verse for months!

The mind ONLY receives and processes information. Information like "Donald Trump is the 45th President of the U.S." or the sun is at the center of our solar system and is responsible for the earth's climate and weather."

I love how John Eldredge describes the heart in his book *Waking the Dead*. I encourage people to read books from authors like him who understand the ways of the heart. Eldredge writes, "*The heart, not the head, wrestles with a deeper reality, and either navigates or drowns in overwhelming waves of convictions and feelings. Your heart toils with the realities around concepts like your son might get killed driving home from school or that you just lost your job and have a wife and kids to take care of.*"

These are not facts that we just receive and file in our head. These things are the true anxieties, joys, or turmoil that can shake us to our very core. They might sometimes compel us to do something crazy or something amazing!

Our emotions are the voice of our hearts and if we do not recognize and process them, they will direct our lives.

These unprocessed emotions begin to feed our thoughts often negatively. Our thoughts turn into attitudes and attitudes produce our actions.

Have you ever awakened at 2 A.M. with your thoughts racing ninety miles an hour, unable to get relief no matter how hard you've tried to stop them? Those thoughts are birthed from the emotions that have been buried in your heart. Have dreams awakened you that were disturbing even though they seemingly made no sense? Dreams like that can simply be a reminder that we have unprocessed fears and emotions we are ignoring, causing our hearts to struggle.

Suggestions to Journal:

When runaway thoughts disrupt your sleep – ask yourself:

"God, what's going on in my heart that I'm afraid about, or feeling guilty about?"

Then put words to those fears:

"What am I afraid of if that happens?"

Is this a fear I've had for a long time? Perhaps even since childhood?

Do my fears connect to a lack of SECURITY? Financial, relational, emotional?

Get to know yourself on a heart level by checking in with yourself when you feel an emotional shift happening within, asking God to help with the question, "What am I feeling?"

BLOCKAGES TO LIVING FROM THE HEART

Where are we living our lives from? It's not unusual to look outside ourselves for successes, possessions, or significant people (authority figures) to validate us.

In fact, the world teaches us that way, and sadly sometimes even the church, so for most of us it has been the only way to live especially since we never felt validated or enough within ourselves.

Our truest lives are meant to originate from our hearts connecting with Christ inside of us and receiving, on a heart level, God's amazing, unconditional love for us. But if we are internally blocked through some past wounds in our hearts that were not healed, and just buried, no matter how much we know that truth of God's love in our minds, we are unable to tap into it and live from it.

You cannot put a truth on top of a lie and expect the truth to remain. The lie must be uprooted and removed first.

We have all received lies or false beliefs through the pain we've experienced. That's why no matter how much truth you've read in the Bible or heard in church, it only lasts for a short time and then the anger, anxiety, fear, or guilt, once again returns. We need to cooperate with the work and desire of God's Spirit to take out the trash (the lies) we've accumulated throughout a lifetime of broken-world living!

The blockages that prevent us from experiencing God's and others' love deeply in our hearts are like trash that has been thrown in the stream of our lives. Without realizing it, the emotionally painful experiences we've had throughout the years have blocked up the flow, and until we are willing to unearth and get out of agreement with the garbage, we are unknowingly affected by it on a continual basis.

Unforgiveness in our heart is another blockage that covers and hardens our hearts with self-protective strategies. Many have forgiven from their head while their heart is still harboring resentment. A clue is when we have an emotional reaction any time the person's name is mentioned. We might even have whole "people groups" that we need to forgive, such as: The Church, Our Parents, Men, Women, Politicians, or Authority Figures.

ASK YOURSELF:

What are my emotions telling me about where my heart might have been wounded or stuck?

For many, anger is their go-to emotion and the only one they feel. Anger is like a lid on the box. We must face the anger we feel, but then invite God to help us look beneath the lid of anger into the box -- what hurtful emotions are lurking in the box?

Example: Fear, disappointments, rejections, sorrow, etc.

Since our anger is a covering emotion, and a go-to response that makes us feel more powerful, what does it cover in you?

I feel angry because

I feel hurt because

How do I feel hurt (list your emotions) Is fear driving my anger?

Do I feel powerless?

Do I feel Helpless? How so?

Fearful of what?

Am I overwhelmed?

Do I feel like I don't have what it takes?

The following partial list of emotions is a good tool to use when putting words to how we feel.

A PARTIAL LIST OF EMOTIONS

- Categories of Emotions and Some of the Subtle Ways They Can Be Experienced
- HURT: Feeling wounded, distressed, offended, injured, abused, used, harmed, pained, sorrowful, suffering, grieved, sad, brokenhearted, disappointed, discouraged, rejected, abandoned, shamed
- FEAR: Feeling anxious, panic, terror, apprehension, alarm, afraid, suspicious, distrusting, worried, over-concerned, troubled, uneasy, anguished, agitated, disquieted, unbelieving
- ANGER: Feeling rage-full, aggressive, depressed (anger turned inward), rebellious, resentful, bitter, desire to punish, frustrated, contemptuous, disrespectful, hostile, annoyed, furious, argumentative, combative, sulky, irritated, outraged, arrogant, antagonizing, overwhelmed, misunderstood, unappreciated, powerless (can fuel anger), having inward or outward tantrums
- GUILT (REAL OR FALSE): Feeling judgmental, critical, envious, always feeling guilty, wanting to hide, disgraceful, disconnected, powerless, isolated, self-condemning
- SHAME (REAL OR FALSE): Feeling insignificant, worthless, a failure, unworthy, embarrassed, unimportant, unwanted, useless, self-sabotaging, forgotten, forsaken, inadequate, insecure, not valuable, discarded, unneeded, disgraceful, self-depreciating, invisible, wanting to hide behind a false self (wearing a mask)
- GRIEF: Feeling sad, sorrowful, undone, distracted, withdrawn, angry, tearful, brokenhearted, overwhelmed

When we believe our performance equals our worth we can never rest. We often find ourselves struggling with pride or the fear of failure along with the fear of being shamed. Unfortunately we usually don't even recognize those emotions because they hide underground. Yet we still feel driven to do and do and do, produce, hold it all together, or control our life and the lives of those around us.

One extremely competent woman I met with never realized how much she had hidden herself in perfectionism and performance until the marriage she had desperately been holding together fell apart. Our pain has a way of breaking our denial and stripping away the facade we have created. As a result of the circumstances, she literally became emotionally unglued because her "performance" was the glue holding it all together.

There can often be a drive to keep it all going, for if we stop spinning the plates, what might happen? The fear of our world falling apart, fear of failure, fear of exposure, fear of loss, or fear of shame is silently lurking. We try to control—God, people, circumstances, ourselves. Anxiety is often then a companion, and unfortunately far too often, that's all we are aware of feeling. We are simply not in touch with the feelings or patterns that are hiding beneath the anxiety.

Buried and denied hurts can produce control. Fear of more hurt can drive the control. Control often produces anxiety. Anxiety then can cause us to keep trying to perform perfectly — all done to keep our lives from falling apart and being seen as a failure.

The answer is to face our fears and put specific words to them. We also need to be willing to struggle through and release those fears in surrender to God who does indeed hold all things together. Colossians 1:17 says, *"He is before all things, and in him all things hold together."*

Walk into your fear, otherwise it will chase you

INVITE GOD TO SHOW YOU:

- What am I afraid will happen if I don't perform well?

- Think about your original home life -- was your acceptance based on your performance that had unrealistic expectations attached to them?

THE MASKS WE WEAR

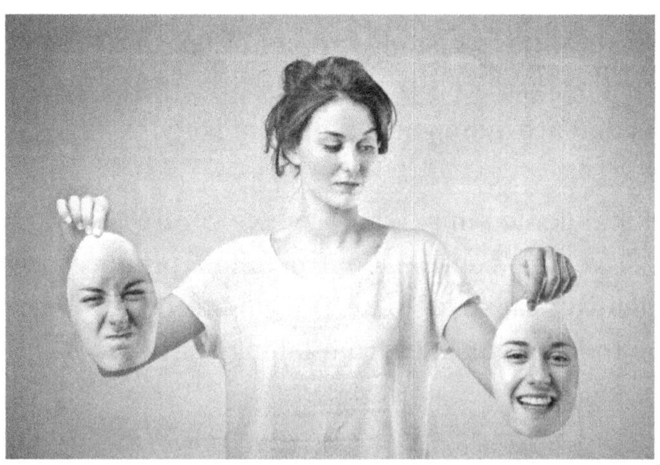

When we are afraid to know ourselves and be known on any deep level, we wear a "mask" to cover ourselves. Once we deem those parts of ourselves unacceptable or incompetent we begin to hide behind masks.

Masks such as:

- perfectionism
- accomplishments
- success
- possessions and wealth
- beauty
- strength
- intellectualism
- super-spirituality or religiosity
- humor

A mask is the false self we create to present to others -- one that we consider more acceptable than who we actually are.

I hear many people complain that people ignore them in a group, or continually reject them. It's as if they don't matter or are invisible. Those same people unfortunately, carry an atmosphere that creates a "wall" with an invisible sign that silently says, "Stay away, don't come near." At the same time there are others who have a "welcoming" spirit that draws people to them.

If you are dissatisfied with everything around you, it usually comes from deep dissatisfaction within. This can play out by wanting to distance ourselves from our struggling relationships, in wanting to leave locations, change jobs, find other churches -- all with the belief that if we can just escape the situation, our lives will go well. The problem is that we bring our systems of survival with us -- we can't escape ourselves! Some others will remain in the situation, but just escape internally or 'shut down.'

ASK YOURSELF:

Am I willing to face myself (instead of escaping) by inviting the Holy Spirit to reveal what is really going on beneath the surface?

God might begin to show you by bringing back memories from very early on, or you might begin to recognize an atmosphere you grew up in that formed a belief system about yourself.

It's not just remembering the memories or the atmosphere that will heal you, but connecting with the emotions you felt as a result. Then invite Jesus, who wrestled with his own emotions as well (in the Garden of Gethsemane, for example) to meet you in the midst of them with his healing.

- What did I feel in my home growing up? Did I feel valued, enjoyed, protected?

- Or did I feel rejected, overlooked, invisible, emotionally abandoned, discarded?

- What was the atmosphere of the home like?

- Was it affirming, welcoming, caring? Or rejecting, shaming, aloof?

- Do you desire to be loved or admired? Why?

- Are you afraid to be truly known? If so, why?

- What do you believe people will see if they really know you?

- In this regard, what am I really afraid of? (try to put words to your feelings)
  I am afraid of_______________________

CONNECTION WITH THE PAIN OF YOUR OWN HEART

We don't like to look inside... Why? The truth is many of us are afraid of what we might find. It's far easier to try to clean up the outside of the cup, but Jesus tells us in Matthew 23:26, *"First clean the inside of the cup and dish, and then the outside also will be clean."*

Life is to be lived from the inside out, not from the outside in, contrary to the way most of us were taught to live. We cannot really get our true lives from outside of us no matter how hard we try because true life is lived from the heart (inside) and released through us to the outside.

We can't get our real lives from people's acceptance, success, money, possessions, fame, or any other thing outside of ourselves.

We bring ourselves to people, we don't get ourselves from people.

Unfortunately, many of us have actually been living the journey someone else has mapped out for us. In order to figure it all out, we sometimes have to enlist the help of a wise counselor or friend who is on their own pilgrimage, but might just be a few steps ahead of us.

However, you can help yourself by being willing to ask some deep questions to your own heart as well.

ASK GOD TO HELP YOU DISCOVER:

- Am I living someone else's plans for me or my own deepest desires?

- If another's plans, why?

- What are my desires? What brings me joy?

- If I have refused to live out of another's control, have I chosen rebellion instead of discovering my true heart's desires? Why?

PART TWO: ENTERING THE BATTLE OVER MY LIFE

The plans of the enemy are very clear when it comes to our lives. The enemy is a thief, a liar. His goal is clearly to destroy you and me. *"The thief comes only to steal and kill and destroy; I have come that they may have life, and have it to the full"* (John 10:10 NIV).

But God had a plan for us before we were even born!

Psalm 139:13-16 says, *"For you created my inmost being; you knit me together in my mother's womb. I praise you because I am fearfully and wonderfully made; your works are wonderful, I know that full well. My frame was not hidden from you when I was made in the secret place, when I was woven together in the depths of the earth. Your eyes saw my unformed body; all the days ordained for me were written in your book before one of them came to be."*

God knew you before your parents did and before the robbery of a broken world stole the fullness of those days!

God says, *"For I, the LORD, love justice; I hate robbery and wrongdoing. In my faithfulness I will reward my people and make an everlasting covenant with them"* (Isaiah 61:8 NIV).

If we are to ever have the life Jesus paid for, not just in heaven, but on this earth, we must fight for it. That is not a fight *against* people or circumstances, but a fight *for* life, *for* our true lives, *for* the heart that no one has ever fought for or truly pursued.

Jesus fought for and pursued our hearts. Yet even that is not enough until we join *with* him fighting *for* the real us. When we join the fight with him, it brings a deeper intimacy with Jesus and gives us the opportunity to co-labor with God's original purposes for our lives. The purposes for which we were created!

ASK YOURSELF:

- What do I do when I am angry?
- What do I feel deep down underneath the anger?

We need our anger, it is our passion! With it we are able to fight for our true lives, rather than waste it fighting against those who have wounded us. Judgment is God's.

- Do I use my anger to blame, shame, or judge myself or another?

- Do I fight against my own heart? If so, how?

- Or do I use my anger for good and fight *for* life for my heart?

INNER LIES

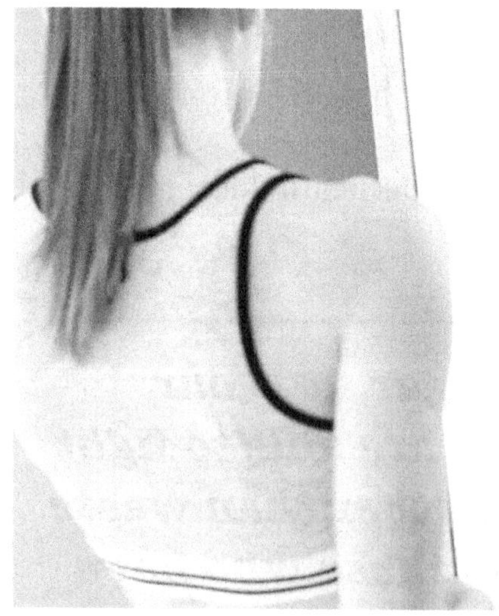

When we have past unhealed wounds they contribute to:

- feeling insignificant
- unsatisfied neediness
- being performance driven
- being consumed with false guilt
- struggling with feelings of loneliness
- past or present rejections
- emotional abandonment experiences
- failures, shaming words and situations

My older sister suffered from bulimia for 20 years. It is a horrible disease because the person can be 80 lbs, be skin and bones, hair falling out due to malnourishment, and they still believe they are fat. The lie feels so true in the face of the dramatic evidence.

Wounds that have been trapped in our souls can make our lies feel very true and cause us to look to external things such as:

- others to approve of us
- success to define us
- possessions to validate us
- people to fill our void when we are lonely

ASK YOURSELF:

- How do you view yourself?

- What are some of the adjectives you use toward yourself when you make a mistake?

- Are they shaming words or redeeming words?

- How do you feel when complimented?

- Can you internally receive the compliment?

TRAPPED IN OUR EMOTIONS

Unhealed Emotional Hurt (Experiences of past pain) that has been lodged in the heart can lead to **heart beliefs** that are usually not accurate, and can be very different than the truths we believe intellectually. Those tormenting heart beliefs can lead to certain **thoughts** that can disturb our peace.

That can then lead us to **destructive actions**, false perceptions, self-protective, arrogant, or sabotaging behaviors that damage our relationships and even our health.

To help discover those buried wounds that continue to affect your life:

Look for set-ups or triggers when you overreact to situations, times when you feel threatened and trapped in anger, or fear. The set-up reveals where we are stuck.

What is a set-up?

A set-up is a trigger that God uses to disrupt us emotionally.

Do you ever find yourself overreacting to a circumstance, a comment, a happening that is way out of proportion to the circumstance? This is an example of a set-up.

God's purpose for the set-up is to disrupt us in order to get our attention, invite us to cooperate with him so he can heal us, and to reveal an unhealthy root within. Instead, we usually get angry and blame! We often want to blame the person who triggered us, ourselves, the circumstance that created the disruption, or even God himself— because we reason, he could have stopped it!

When you find yourself overreacting to a comment, what has that triggered in you from the past?

God uses set-ups to disrupt us from our false ways of surviving life. These false ways feel right to us at the time, but are preventing us from living a life of true peace and freedom.

Proverbs 16:25, says, *"There is a way that seems right to a man, but in the end it leads to death."*

It sometimes takes a disruption of one kind or another to make us desperate enough to get off that slow train of deadness, dullness, just settling, or boredom. Sadly too many people's lives become about just plain survival.

The disruption could be something like a job loss, a serious relationship problem, an illness, financial difficulty, or any other circumstance that disrupts us by shaking our ability to manage the world we live in. For some it might be that you simply feel overwhelmed, weary, or that dullness or depression sets in, and you just can't do it all anymore. I had to see that life, as I had tried to arrange it, just wasn't working. In fact, I was making a terrible mess of everything that I was simply trying to hold together!

It is easy to see any of those as a negative situation, but disruptions are often necessary for us to no longer remain in a state of being lost or trying to control. If we can fight the urge to not hide in depression or just blame someone or something in our negative circumstances, we could find the courage to face the feelings that begin to surface. Yes, they are being triggered in the present situation, but what are they attached to?

ASK YOURSELF:

- Am I struggling with anxiety, the fear of being out of control, the fear of failure, being shamed, or possibly powerlessness?

- Do I struggle with trying to control circumstances, others, myself, my relationships, my work, my health, my finances?

- What do I fear if I can't be in control?

- What am I trying to prove? To whom?

- If my world, as I've designed it falls apart, what do I fear will happen?

- What are the buttons that get pushed in me, and why?

- Where am I afraid to risk? or where do I not have my voice?

Invite the Spirit of God to uncover any hidden wound that is getting triggered. However, be aware that when it gets to the surface, you will probably feel emotional pain. When that pain begins to surface, don't run from it, but meet Jesus there. He also suffered similar feelings in his time on this earth.

I love interpreting others' dreams, but I almost never can interpret my own. The same is true with discovering our deepest buried emotions, especially in the beginning. Things that we struggle to make sense of, others like counselors or mentors, can sometimes be very helpful in enabling us to see. The goal is healing and freedom and sometimes we need outside help getting there. The first help we need is from the Helper, the wonderful Counselor, the Healer himself whose mission it was to set the captives free and heal the broken-hearted, but he also desires to invite us to join him in bringing that freedom to others.

Isaiah 60:1 NIV says, *"The Spirit of the Sovereign LORD is on me, because the LORD has anointed me to proclaim good news to the poor. He has sent me to bind up the brokenhearted, to proclaim freedom for the captives and release from darkness for the prisoners..."*

Allowing others to help us along our healing journey can be very humbling, but at the same time wonderfully healing.

- If it is difficult for you to humbly ask for the help of a friend or a counselor as you begin this journey of healing, ask yourself why.

- Could there be a buried heart belief that there's something wrong with you if you need help?

"Therefore confess your faults to each other and pray for each other so that you may be healed. The prayer of a righteous person is powerful and effective" (James 5:16).

Many people feel false shame because of needing the help of another, but that is simply the way we've been created. Asking for help is allowing ourselves to be human, and is not something we are meant to feel shameful about.

As God is a God of light and not darkness, our healing also takes place in the light, and not through continuing to hide ourselves in denial because of false shame.

GETTING TO KNOW YOURSELF

When struggling with anger, guilt, shame, or fear, or when you find yourself overreacting to a situation, invite the Holy Spirit to help you discover:

- What was the feeling in the present situation that just got triggered?

- When have I felt this way before?

(Maybe the feeling goes back to early childhood or any time thereafter)

- What fear might this be triggering in me?

"I am afraid of___________."

- What beliefs about myself, others, God, and life did I pick up from that earlier wound?

- How is it still affecting my life? In what ways?

Example: If there was rejection, what did I falsely "learn" about myself, my life, others, God, through that rejection?

The pain we feel when we experience rejection is shame and the lie we pick up is something like: "I am not worthy of being loved," or "I am not acceptable," or "I am a failure," or any variation of that.

- Could that buried rejection, betrayal, abuse, emotional abandonment or shame still be controlling how I might be afraid to trust, risk, value myself, or have a voice with others?

- Has it caused me to try to control myself, others, circumstances, God? How?

LOVING OURSELVES

Jesus said we will love others as we love ourselves, but if we've been wounded, as all of us have in this broken world, chances are we are unable to truly love ourselves on the deepest level of our hearts even though we have the head knowledge.

We are caught between two beliefs.

Our hearts have been wounded so we don't experience God's love deeply in there, but our head knows what the Bible says. Unfortunately, there becomes a "disconnect" on the inside of us and we are unable to flow from within the core of ourselves.

As a result, we are constantly looking for validation and worth from outside ourselves. The way out of this dilemma is to be willing to allow God to search us from within and show us the wounded ways that have tripped us up and robbed our lives and relationships.

"Search me, God, and know my heart; test me and know my anxious thoughts. See if there is any offensive way in me, and lead me in the way everlasting" (Psalm 139:23-24 NIV).

It is not uncommon for committed Christians to carry anger at God when he hasn't come through for them in the past in the way they desired and prayed. All too often they are not even aware of their anger at God and vehemently deny even having it.

Anger towards God must be faced, owned, and honestly struggled with. Any religious spirit that keeps a person in denial must be broken, and blame must be finally released through the process. If this does not happen, healing is thwarted and he remains in bondage on a heart level.

A mask then often replaces true, intimate heart connection and they too often give God a cold shoulder or just 'go through the motions' of serving God. Some people are unable to really trust God on any deep heart level, and usually simply ignore him or just serve Him religiously.

There can also be buried anger at God that goes all the way back to the original hurt that might have occurred way back in childhood.

An example of that might be when a child buries the anger and blame they had at God from when their Christian parents divorced, or from any abusive situation they experienced early on.

Their angry question is usually, "God, why didn't you stop it?". If there had been no one there at the time to help them process that anger, it can remain tucked away inside of them only to surface unexpectedly, and often at an inappropriate person.

For example, it can be buried anger originally at a parent that then gets inappropriately aimed and displaced on a spouse when triggered in the present. I did that with my husband even though his character and behavior was nothing like my father's. It's important to allow yourself to honestly struggle from the deepest part of your heart with questions like:

- Where were you God when that happened to me?
- God, do you care?
- If I let go of my anger and the self-protection it gives me, God, are you enough to keep me from being emotionally destroyed?

Allow your heart to be honest with God because he already knows what is lurking within us and is not shocked. He desires our false conclusions to be brought to the light so we can work the feelings through to an ultimate surrender in trust to him and his ways.

"And we know that in all things God works for the good of those who love him, who have been called according to his purpose" (Romans 8:28 NIV).

ROOTS

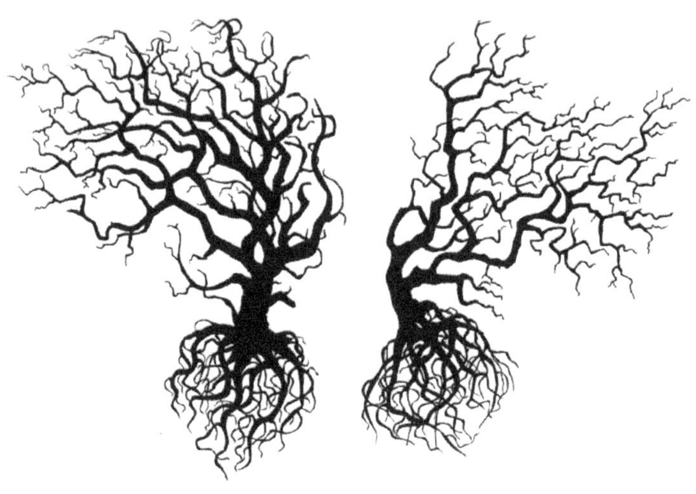

We all have a root system beneath the surface or on the interior of our lives. If that root system has been recognized and healed where necessary, we will be like a healthy "tree" that produces good, healthy fruit.

Yet many of us have had our root systems twisted without even realizing it. It seems however, we can always find someone with more dysfunction with whom it's easy to compare ourselves so that we end up looking pretty good. Growing up, a particular member of my family appeared quite dysfunctional in their actions. I actually prided myself at the time for not being like them, until I sadly realized I was a "functional dysfunctional" instead of a "dysfunctional dysfunctional". It's all the same, the one just looks and performs better on the outside!

The twisting within us can come from:

- Traumas or wounds we experience early in life that have never been addressed or healed
- The dysfunctional ways we have been brought up
- The negative, fearful, or shaming atmosphere of our childhood home
- Words spoken to us that wounded us on a deep level of the heart
- Emotional disconnection or abandonment from key people in our lives
- Rejections that we have experienced
- Shaming experiences

ASK YOURSELF:

- Do I feel stuck overreacting to the same issues or emotions surfacing over and over?

- Is there a particular area in which I just seem to continually go around the same mountain?

- Is there a relationship or area in which I seem to sabotage or trip myself up?

- Are there certain people I feel discomfort or shame around?

- Do I feel hopeless or powerless in any area?

FRUIT

Jesus said we would really know people by the fruit they bring forth from within, and that includes ourselves.

Well-meaning spoken words mean very little if the fruit of a person's life remains bad. For example how many, "I'm sorry's" have been spoken that actually have never borne any good fruit of change. There is a huge difference between a lifeless

Christmas tree that is beautifully decorated, and a fruit tree that doesn't look like much when in its infancy, but later produces life-giving fruit that feeds others.

"But the fruit of the Spirit is love, joy, peace, patience, kindness, goodness, faithfulness, gentleness, self-control..." (Galatians 5:22-23 NASB)

Invite the Spirit of God to show you the fruit in your own life.

ASK GOD:

- What kind of fruit is my life bringing forth?
- Is this fruit healthy or unhealthy for my life and relationships?

The following are all good fruit of a healthy root system.

- good character
- integrity
- kindness
- openness
- honesty
- patience
- perseverance

UNHEALTHY ROOTS BEAR UNHEALTHY FRUIT

Fruit grows from the inside out so that means if we have developed an unhealthy root system within us, it must be faced and dealt with. Good roots produce good, healthy fruit, and unhealthy roots, bad fruit.

Jesus said, *"By their fruit you will recognize them. Do people pick grapes from thorn-bushes, or figs from thistles? Likewise, every good tree bears good fruit, but a bad tree bears bad fruit.*

"Make a tree good and its fruit will be good, or make a tree bad and its fruit will be bad, for a tree is recognized by its fruit. ...For the mouth speaks what the heart is full of. A good man brings good things out of the good stored up in him, and an evil man brings evil things out of the evil stored up in him" (Matthew 7:16-17 NIV).

Bad fruit can affect our character, our way of relating, causing us to dishonor and disrespect others. It can cause us to have little integrity or to be selfish instead of self-caring in a healthy way. It can create a critical spirit, blame, judgments, greed, avoidance, lack of peace, and a demanding heart, to name just a few of the ways it affects us.

Wounded people wound others, healed people release health and encouragement to others.

When someone has a faulty internal root system, they can sometimes seem very nice on the surface, but nice is simply something we can put on like a mask. Usually something is going on completely different in their hearts.

Niceness and kindness are two very different things. Kindness is a fruit of the Spirit that grows from within the heart through our surrender to God's Spirit within us. Niceness is something we can simply take on and off like a mask.

If the root that has grown within us is still twisted, we will have limited genuine fruit coming out of our hearts. And Jesus reminds us that our words and actions come from our hearts whether they are good or bad.

In today's society, there has arisen a belief that you can mildly put down, use, or abuse someone, then just say you're sorry, and move on. The one who apologizes might seem to have some short-term remorse and behavioral change, but it's not lasting because it doesn't stem from their heart. Behavioral change that does not come from true repentance of the heart, rarely lasts more than two weeks.

Bad fruit can even consist of very subtle demeaning or putting another down that sometimes comes in the form of a joke or sarcasm. The name for that survival system is *contempt* which is actually a disdain and lack of respect for the other person. When we use contempt on someone, it usually has a hidden purpose. For example, contempt covers any shame we fear coming toward us, throws it back on the other, and deadens any longings we might have had to be loved and enjoyed by them through shutting them down with disdain.

Proverbs 26:18-19 AMP, describes that contemptuous mask as being *"like a madman who throws firebrands, arrows, and death; so is the man who deceives his neighbor (acquaintance, friend) And then says, "Was I not joking?"*

Some examples of contempt:

Spoken words that put another down, use of painful sarcasm, having a poorly disguised attitude, a disgusted sigh, the rolling of the eyes, or a shaming look that hurts the other, but then is quickly dismissed or excused. Sometimes a person will accuse the wounded one of having caused their anger and contempt.

Some more examples of bad fruit coming from an unhealthy root:

- An abusive accusation that declares, "You made me do it!" That is a shaming accusation and is the true shame of the accuser, not one who is the victim of it.
- Using another person for our own purposes to get what we need from them.

- Taking thoughtless advantage of others and selfishly only seeing ourselves and our own agendas. That is disregarding them as people to be respected and valued.
- Unhealthy fruit can create an atmosphere around us that keeps others out, instead of being a welcoming one.

PART THREE:
YOUR YOUNGER SELF

When we have been significantly wounded as children with no one to help us make sense of our emotions and work them through, they get buried, denied, and locked away in an internal "closet" of our own making. We continue living and growing in other areas of our lives, but it's like that particular emotion, or several emotions, get locked away within us.

As life happens to us, and those emotions get triggered in our present circumstances, we tend to over-react because the original buried emotion leaks out from under the locked door. So now we have the emotional response from the past beneath the one we are experiencing in the present and we are emotionally transported back to reacting from the age of that original wound.

An argument then between a married couple, for example, often descends into a fight between two four-year olds trying to be heard! The buried wound however, is not always from a childhood hurt, and can be from any age where there was a significant wound, even from the beginning of their relationship. If the emotions were not faced, worked through, healed, and released through forgiving the other, then the wound remains unresolved, and can cause hurt in the present.

For example, this often plays out in marriages or other relationships when we have experienced disappointments and hurts early on that were never truly worked through and were simply buried under the carpet.

Over the years the resentments build, one on top of another, until we have eventually developed a wall around our hearts. We might go through the motions of relating, usually about superficial things and the necessities of living together, but a door to the heart has been shut that allows true connecting and emotional vulnerability. Then in an argument, a litany of old resentments and disappointments come barreling out!

There can be past rejections in a young man's life that have shut down portions of his heart coming from various girls with whom he desired to develop relationships. Then when the right one comes along, he holds back, or is afraid to risk in the relationship. He sabotages the very thing he longs to experience.

Without the healing of earlier rejections, a young woman can begin to focus only on the external, creating an image, maybe beautiful on the outside, but never really known on any deep level of her heart because that got shut down long before.

True beauty comes from within us; first spirit, then soul, and then body. In order for that life-giving harmony to come forth from within us however, there must be a facing and healing of the original wounds.

Past buried hurts not faced and healed can keep us playing it safe, hugging the shore, afraid to risk in various important areas that affect our present lives.

- In relationships — it can cause us to be fearful and want to dominate and control a relationship. Or even while desiring closer connection, it can cause someone to appear aloof, disengaged, cold, and uninviting.
- In an area like finances -- it can cause greed, foolish spending or stinginess, holding back and not being able to enjoy the fruits of our labors.

- In business, it can actually prevent success because of being reticent, disengaged, and cause a lack of motivation.

ASK YOURSELF:

In what areas am I "playing it safe" due to past buried hurts?

Those buried wounds can cause us to live out of the impulsiveness of the child buried within and make very foolish decisions. Whenever I'm tempted with impulsiveness in a situation, it becomes a red flag for me that I'm acting out of the child in me instead of my adult self.

SHAME

Since the pain we feel when rejected or abandoned is shame with the lie that tells us we are not sufficient or acceptable, we need to take a look at shame itself if we are to get out of agreement with its message.

There are two kinds of shame:

Legitimate (true shame) is healthy shame. That shame tells us we have hurt or offended someone, or in some way come short of God's glory through our selfish choices. It is our own legitimate shame that we confess and bring to the cross for forgiveness. Real shame that is owned is clean because when we confess our sins, he forgives and cleanses us. (1 John 1:9)

Illegitimate or false shame belongs to another. It is not ours. It actually belongs to someone else due to their own sin. It came from something that was done *to us* by another.

An example of this is abuse of any kind. It is never the fault of the one who has been abused. That shame belongs to the one doing the abusing, but sadly, without understanding this, the one who has been abused carries it illegitimately. That shame needs to be released and the message it carries gotten out of agreement with.

Another example would be when a parent disciplines a child through guilting or shaming. That is the parent's shame, not the child's, and sadly the child then illegitimately often carries false guilt like a heavy coat over them that they can never shed. As an adult, they feel guilty over everything. At the same time though, they don't usually learn to take legitimate responsibility for their own actions.

ASK YOURSELF:

- What illegitimate shame might I be carrying from someone else's actions toward me?
- Is there any legitimate shame that I'm still carrying that I need to bring to the cross in order to receive forgiveness?

"If we confess our sins, he is faithful and just and will forgive us our sins and purify us from all unrighteousness" (1 John 1:9 NIV).

- What was the false message I "learned" about myself from any rejection or shaming I might have experienced?

For example, LIES like: "I don't measure up." "I'm a failure."

I personally learned the lie that I was just a piece of garbage, a throw away, so I desperately tried to keep that secret hidden without even realizing I had the secret. It was not done consciously because the denial of the lie was buried so deeply within myself.

- Could your lie have been something like, "I am not acceptable," "I am not valuable," "I am not enough," "I am not worthwhile," or "I am a failure?"

- Ask yourself, did I pick up a false image of myself, and have I used a mask to cover the shame I felt as a result, so others wouldn't really see me?

- Have I rejected myself or parts of myself because of what I experienced?

- What parts of me have I deemed unacceptable?

- Has it caused me to try to prove myself to others to get acceptance?

- Perhaps even through my performance, appearance, or perfectionism?

- Or the opposite, has it caused me to not try very hard at things, to hide myself?
- Have I sabotaged my success in any area? Perhaps in work, school, my relationships, etc.?

"Instead of your shame you will receive a double portion, and instead of disgrace you will rejoice in your inheritance. And so you will inherit a double portion in your land, and everlasting joy will be yours" (Isaiah 61:7 NIV).

GRIEVING OUR DISAPPOINTMENTS & AWAKENING DESIRE

We have all been disappointed simply through living our lives in a broken world with other broken and wounded people.

We all have places in us where we had hoped.... You fill in the blank. What did your disappointed hope look like? It might have been a desire for a family, a certain career, success, ministry, or for someone who would pursue you. Those desires, when not faced and grieved, can get locked up inside our hearts, scab over, and eventually deaden our hearts.

Some questions to ask:

- Do you feel like you are just existing? Going through the motions of living, but are not really alive?

- Has your disappointment turned to resentment, perhaps of others who appear to have achieved?
- Do you feel disregarded -- by others, or perhaps God?
- I suggest you make a list of your disappointed desires in as many areas as you are able.

Our hearts get buried in the graveyard of those disappointed longings and desires and if we don't face and grieve them, we lose the deepest part of us. We lose our passion, our longings, our vitality. Grieving our disappointed desires allows our deepest longings to begin to surface and be experienced. Yes, this is a broken world and so it's not first about obtaining the fulfillment of them, but of having them. They belong to us and they have been robbed. We need our longings back even if they have been disappointed; they must be grieved if we are to live fully alive.

We will always live with an ache, a groan on some level for we were created for the perfect world, the Garden, and this is not it! But we will also live with alive hearts and can then begin to cooperate and co-labor with God from our deepest hearts in ways we never thought possible. We become passionate people who can taste and see that God is good. Grieving our losses enables us to receive and delight in God's good gifts, even the tiniest ones, in ways that were formerly impossible. In this broken world, we will always experience both gifts and losses, sometimes in the same five minutes!

"We know that the whole creation has been groaning as in the pains of childbirth right up to the present time. Not only so, but we ourselves, who have the firstfruits of the Spirit, groan

inwardly as we wait eagerly for our adoption to sonship, the redemption of our bodies" (Romans 8:22-23 NIV).

Understanding Grief

God's natural process of dealing with the disappointed desires and losses of a broken world is to grieve them. However we have many things, both large and small to grieve that go far beyond death and divorce. Major grief takes as long as it takes to get through and we must become patient with the process. But one significant thing many of us have to grieve is the picture we have painted for our own lives, the way we thought our lives would look. That picture we created must be released if we are to begin our true journey with God in his bigger story for us — the one we were originally created to live and that truly satisfies our hearts.

Grief must be owned to be released. It doesn't just go away by itself, instead it goes underground and can surface years later without warning. A woman I worked with had lost her husband five years prior to my meeting her. Her solution at the time of her loss was to just get busy so she never allowed herself the process of working through her pain. Five years later, the grief unexpectedly erupted, putting her life on hold.

My grief after the death of my husband took eleven months. Even though I was committed to working through the grief process, each day as I returned home to my now empty house, I felt the sorrow of my aloneness. Then one day, very unexpectedly, as I walked into my house, I felt joy bubbles rising up within me accompanied by the amazing realization that I enjoyed living alone! However five years later, after a special, prolonged time with extended family, upon arriving home, I experienced a fresh wave of grief as I faced the "all alone" emptiness of the next four days during the holiday season.

Grief is more than just major happenings of death, divorce, or some other major tragedy. In order for us to be relieved of grief we must face our losses. Some small ones, like a disappointing day not turning out the way we wanted, might take just 30 seconds, and are often done unconsciously once we understand this concept.

In a broken world there can be gifts and losses in the same hour. Our lives are not all good or all bad, but have mixture. Once we have learned to grieve and release our losses, we begin to notice tiny gifts all around us that we would never have recognized and enjoyed before — they would have seemed too insignificant, but now they bring us joy!

Some Common Grief Symptoms:

- Tightness or heaviness in the throat or chest
- Denial of the reality of our grief
- Restlessness
- Inability to concentrate, distraction
- Anger at God or our loved one
- Unexpected crying or other emotion, waves of sadness, disappointment
- Physical weakness
- Difficulty with sleep, dreams of the loved one
- Forgetfulness, struggle with memory
- Loss of appetite

- Feeling empty, forsaken, all alone
- Inability to complete simple tasks
- Preoccupation with your loss
- Guilt feelings
- Feeling the need to protect others' feelings while neglecting your own

There are **stages to grief,** and going through them is a process we have to enter instead of avoid.

Depending on the grief material you read, the descriptions vary a bit, but generally they include:

- Shock
- Denial
- Feelings of Betrayal
- Bargaining with God
- Anger, Disappointment, Sorrow
- Acceptance

"Blessed are those who mourn, for they will be comforted" (Matthew 5:4 NIV)

PARTICIPATION WITH JESUS IN THE HEALING OF THE CHILD WITHIN

ASK YOURSELF:

- Where or when did I get wounded in my earlier life?

- Is there a memory of specific pain or was there just an atmosphere of pain I lived in?

Sometimes "our normal" was not really normal at all and we were wounded by it. Perhaps there is nothing you can put your finger on, but in the present when certain things happen, you tend to over-react, maybe with anger, fear, blame, sadness, or feelings of powerlessness.

- What is your particular feeling that gets triggered?

- Ask God to show you when you felt that feeling before. How far does it go back?

- How old do you feel when you are triggered?

- Close your eyes. Can you see that child?

If so, do you desire to move toward or away from, or do you just feel aloof, distanced from them?

Each of those feelings show you how you yourself have treated that part of you.

- Stay with the younger you until you can embrace him/her.

- Are you able to see how you might have also rejected or shamed that wounded part of you with negative self-talk or by simply denying the pain that was originally experienced?

- Can you ask that little child still locked within you for forgiveness for your own rejecting, abandoning and shutting them away just like the others did?

- Will they forgive you?

- Can you see Jesus, the man of sorrows, anywhere there?

Please note: If we are unable to see Jesus there, it usually just shows us how we have shut him out of that part of ourselves as well. You might have felt angry toward him or abandoned by him too.

Parents or other authority figures were meant, in a perfect world, to be a picture of God's love and care for us, but sadly many of us experienced the extreme opposite, so we developed a skewed picture of God.

The Bible describes Jesus as a *"Man of sorrows and acquainted with grief"* (Isaiah 53). He was there weeping for you, for he too experienced the rejection, abandonment, and the hurt of this broken world. He has been patiently knocking on your heart's door, even though you couldn't yet hear his knock.

He has been waiting for the day when you would face the wound and allow him to meet you in the pain with restoration and the healing of your broken heart.

God's natural process of dealing with the disappointed desires and the losses of a broken world is to grieve them. He grieves and weeps with us over the wounds caused by this fallen world. He knocks on our heart's door, longing to be invited into the pain that is still lurking there.

Jesus' Mission says: *"The Spirit of the Lord God is upon me, Because the Lord has anointed and commissioned me to bring good news to the humble and afflicted; He has sent me to bind up [the wounds of] the brokenhearted, To proclaim release [from confinement and condemnation] to the [physical and spiritual] captives and freedom to prisoners"* (Isaiah 61:1 AMP).

- Now can you invite him to embrace that younger part of you? He always waits to be invited into the pain.
- Feel his loving embrace. Taste and see that he is good and a healer of broken hearts.
- Is there anyone back there who wounded you that you might have to forgive and release into his hands?
- Now that younger you needs nurturing and loving care. Will you join Jesus in nurturing him/her back to life? Use the Scriptures below to nurture that younger part of you with loving-kindness.

How you speak to yourself from now on is vitally important, especially when making a mistake. That part of you needs to be lovingly joined with Jesus. Jesus is the lover, Satan the accuser — who will you join forces with on that child's behalf?

SEEING THE TENDER HEART OF JESUS IN THE HEALING PROCESS

Invite Jesus to come over to your little child within and see what happens! When Jesus comes with his warm, loving, accepting, strong embrace, what are you feeling?

Let Jesus take the younger you out of the dark place into his beautiful creation where freedom awaits.

"The Lord is close to the broken-hearted and saves those who are crushed in spirit" (Psalm 34:18).

"But for you who revere my name, the sun of righteousness will rise with healing in its rays. And you will go out and frolic like well-fed calves" (Malachi 4:2 NIV).

"... He will gather the lambs in His arm, He will carry them in His bosom; He will gently and carefully lead those nursing their young" (Isaiah 40:11 AMP).

"What do you think? If a man owns a hundred sheep, and one of them wanders away, will he not leave the ninety-nine on the hills and go to look for the one that wandered off? And if he finds it, truly I tell you, he is happier about that one sheep than about the ninety-nine that did not wander off" (Matthew 18:12-13 NIV).

"Jerusalem, Jerusalem, ...how often I have longed to gather your children together, as a hen gathers her chicks under her wings, and you were not willing" (Matthew 23:37 NIV).

(Jesus has sorrow -- he longs and waits to heal and restore us, but he doesn't do it for us. Instead, He does it with us.)

"Jesus said, 'Let the little children come to me, and do not hinder them, for the kingdom of heaven belongs to such as these'" (Matthew 19:14 NIV).

BECOMING WHOLE

We long to be people of true integrity, people who can be trusted. Integrity comes from the different parts within us becoming integrated into a whole. Then we are not double minded and deceptive, but we begin to find we are more able to walk with the peace of God leading us. We begin to be seen as safe, trustworthy people even though not perfect, still flawed, but generally the motivations of our hearts are becoming clean.

"The integrity of the upright guides them, but the unfaithful are destroyed by their duplicity" (Proverbs 11:3 NIV).

"All a person's ways seem pure to them, but motives are weighed by the LORD" (Proverbs 16:2 NIV).

RECOGNIZING THE REAL

Our lives are meant to be lived authentically, emanating from the heart, which is the center of our being, where Christ in us dwells.

- His life then is able to infiltrate ours
- His life is enabled to come forth through ours in our own flavor of uniqueness and gifting
- His life within ours becomes a life-giving mixture that allows us to freely flow together with his Spirit in harmony
- Him in me, I in Him, together we live

That flow in unity with His life within us is beautiful and life-giving. It brings exhilaration, and joy to us as it blesses and releases life to others. Instead of being drained, we become energized and strengthened in our weakness.

"I have been crucified with Christ and I no longer live, but Christ lives in me*. The life I now live in the body, I live by faith in the Son of God, who loved me and gave Himself for me"* (Galatians 2:20 NIV).

"the mystery that has been kept hidden for ages and generations, but is now disclosed to the Lord's people. To them God has chosen to make known among the Gentiles the glorious riches of this mystery, which is ***Christ in you, the hope of glory****"* (Colossians 1:26-27 NIV).

DENIAL

Denial must be broken and former pain faced concerning the things that have shut our hearts down. Deadness must be dealt with. We choose denial to escape feeling the original pain, disappointed desires, and destroyed hopes.

Denial lies to us about life and tells us we can pretend instead of truly experiencing life and vitality. Even feeling pain is preferable to denial for that is the only way we can truly heal.

It's similar to a physical wound that must be acknowledged before we can tend to it properly and allow it to heal. If you had a wound in your body that you continually ignored, eventually it would cause major health problems.

Caring for it from the beginning would allow it to heal properly, but if that were not the case, at some point it would affect your life in various ways. We are made with a similar design in our souls. Our soul consists of our minds, will, and emotions, and it is in the soul that we have been wounded.

"Dear friend, I pray that you may enjoy good health and that all may go well with you, even as your soul is getting along well" (3 John 1:2 NIV).

FANTASY

Fantasy is one thing that many choose to hide in. In our fantasies, we recreate our world with our own picture of false happiness while denying the reality of what we really feel or have felt in the past. That can happen through magical thinking, daydreaming, pretense, hiding in illusions of reality, living vicariously through movies, novels, video games, pornography, etc.

Living in fantasy can close the heart to true life experience and the wonderful opportunity to meet God even in the messes. When we face the real, we can have intimate relationship with Jesus as we meet him in our pain, within the fellowship of his suffering. He too experienced the pain of this broken world, becoming a compassionate healer of our broken hearts.

"Those who work their land will have abundant food, but those who chase fantasies have no sense" (Proverbs 12:11 NIV).

GIVING UP VICTIMHOOD

We can hide from true life by remaining a victim of our painful circumstances. We do that when we continually blame others or our life circumstances for our struggle. Until we give up the blame and the false victim identity we have created, and forgive the offender from the heart, we remain trapped.

"But you, God, see the trouble of the afflicted; you consider their grief and take it in hand. The **victims** *commit themselves to you; you are the helper of the fatherless"* (Psalm 10:14 NIV).

"Although he was a Son, he learned obedience from what he suffered" (Hebrews 5:8 NIV).

"Therefore confess your sins to each other and pray for each other so that you may be healed. The prayer of a righteous person is powerful and effective" (James 5:16 NIV).

Since this is a journey of the heart, it can sometimes be difficult to walk it alone and there is no shame in inviting a good and safe friend or Christian counselor to walk it with us. Our denial and distancing from our own emotions can be so strong that we need another to pick up on things we might not be seeing.

Psalm 51 tells us that God desires truth in our inmost being. Truth in our minds alone does not heal or free us to become who we were created to be. The Spirit of God desires to search the heart of man, in order to bring hurtful things, still lurking in the past, to the surface. He desires to heal and free us from their hold and continual destruction.

When our hearts begin to heal, we start to be able to flow in harmony from within us. As our hearts connect to truth instead of lies, our minds are renewed with more peace. Our spirits can then begin to rule as directed by God's Spirit of life and truth. As a result, our bodies can begin to experience new well-being, peace, rest, and healing. We begin to flow more harmoniously.

When we have lost touch with our own heart, we have lost our truest self.

Proverbs 4:23 reminds us, *"Above all else, guard your heart, for everything you do flows from it."*

Can you hear how important our hearts are to living our truest lives? But many of us have lost heart and instead began living from outside of it, dictated by the demands of life, others' expectations and opinions, or the world's agenda for us. What happened to our hearts—our true center?

Sadly for many of us, our hearts simply got lost or buried. Very early on in life our hearts got hurt, dismissed, devalued, stepped on, laughed at, rejected, abandoned, and basically just thrown away! How many of us heard mocking words declaring in one way or another, "What's wrong with you, you're too sensitive!" No, we weren't *too* sensitive. We were created that way, and it's a gift not a curse.

We were never guided in how to live with our sensitivity. Most of our families did not know how to shepherd our hearts. They do not understand that life is to be lived from the heart because they have neglected and dismissed their own heart. However, this is not about blaming others, it's about recognizing how lost we really are on the deepest level of our heart, and being willing to fight to get our heart back.

Our feelings are the voice of our hearts.

Those uncomfortable emotions are not our hearts but instead they are a voice telling us where our hearts are struggling. They are reminding us we are not listening to our hearts, but trying to live our lives from a different, very lifeless source outside of ourselves.

When we feel separated from God and disconnected from him, why is that? We have simply distanced ourselves from our own hearts where God lives. That often comes when we haven't understood his ways in a particular circumstance. Are we perhaps angry or disappointed, but not wrestling through those particular emotions with him? We might have to ask God, "Where were you when this happened?" When we reconnect with our hearts, guess who is waiting for us? He never left, we did!

One thing I find to be a good tool of reconnection is writing-- to write out our truest feelings, the good, the bad, and the ugly. God knows it all anyway, but he wants us to be honest with Him and not just pious and religious! God loves the real—He designed us that way. All connected relationships are designed to be on a firm foundation of a willingness to be open, honest, and trusting. This also includes our relationship with ourselves as well as with God.

If we are to have intimacy with God's heart, we must first learn intimacy with our own hearts.

Intimacy = into-me-see

Discovering the feelings of our own hearts, connecting from that level of intimacy with God's heart, enables us to have true intimacy with the hearts of others.

"Search me, O God, and know my heart; test me and know my anxious thoughts" (Psalm 139:23).

We all long to be seen, heard, and known, and we often get angry because others don't "get us." The truth is, we are trying to get our identity and value from other people. We look outside of ourselves, instead of discovering who we really are and bringing ourselves to them. Who was it that God originally created us to be before the robbery of living in a broken world with broken people?

"You have searched me, LORD, and you know me" (Psalm 139:1 NIV).

God longs to introduce us to our real selves, the one he knew prior to our birth and the robbery of this broken world. He knew us before our parents did!

"For you created my inmost being; you knit me together in my mother's womb. I praise you because I am fearfully and wonderfully made; your works are wonderful, I know that full well. My frame was not hidden from you when I was made in the secret place, when I was woven together in the depths of the earth. Your eyes saw my unformed body; all the days ordained for me were written in your book before one of them came to be" Psalm 139:13-16 NIV).

When we really discover our true selves, we can bring ourselves to others instead of trying to get ourselves from them.

REAL WORTH, REAL LIFE

Our worth comes from God, Himself, Who created us in His own likeness, who saw and knew us before our parents did, and who actually even called us into being. As we begin to receive the worth that Jesus Himself saw as he hung on that cross to purchase us back, we begin to recognize that yes, I am a "pearl of great price!" Amazingly, He was willing to give up all to buy us back from the robbery!

You are here on purpose, wonderfully created for God's delightful purposes to be brought forth in you. They are the purposes that truly satisfy us on the deepest level of our hearts. *"For we are His workmanship, created in Christ Jesus for good works, which God prepared beforehand so that we would walk in them"* (Ephesians 2:10). *"For You formed my inward parts; You wove me in my mother's womb. I will give thanks to You, for I am fearfully and wonderfully made; wonderful are Your works, and my soul knows it very well"* (Psalm 139:13).

Your eyes have seen my unformed substance; And in Your book were all written the days that were ordained for me, When as yet there was not one of them" (Psalms 139:13-14). Those are the days that were ordained for you, and now you must fight to get back that which was taken from you!

Genesis 2:7 says, *"it was the breath of God breathed into the clay of the earth that made us a living being."* Then in verse 15, *"God put man in the garden to do."* It is still the breath of God released into our flesh that gives us **identity**, not our performance, no matter how good that might be! When we receive into ourselves His breath of life that gives us our identity, our "doing" becomes tending, not toiling. Toiling was part of the curse (Genesis 3:17-19).

We do not have to be under the toil of the curse anymore!

"Christ redeemed us from the curse of the law by becoming a curse for us, for it is written, 'Cursed is everyone who is hung on a tree'" (Galatians 3:13).

Through our personal acceptance of the work Jesus completed on the cross and his resurrection from the dead, we are in the process of cooperating with God's Spirit in being restored to God's original worth, value and intent for us on this earth. It takes our inviting the Spirit of God into our formerly buried, hurt-filled places if we are to deeply co-labor with him in the restoration process. That brings resurrection life to our broken hearts!

It is His resurrection life revealed in us, combined with our own uniqueness, that gives us life, worth, and purpose. Our *doing* is meant to come out of that secure place of *being* the true selves God originally had in mind when he created us with His great love and value. However we will be constantly thwarted in becoming our true selves if we still have significant unhealed wounds within.

"He who believes in Me [who adheres to, trusts in, and relies on Me], as the Scripture has said, 'From his innermost being will flow continually rivers of living water" (John 7:38 AMP).

In order to begin to know your true self, ask God to help you discover:

- What do I really love?
- What brings me life when I do it?
- Make a list of at least 5 things that you love—things that light you up when you do them.
  What do they have in common?

"The Spirit of the Sovereign Lord is on me, because the Lord has anointed me to proclaim good news to the poor. He has sent me to bind up the brokenhearted, to proclaim freedom for the captives and release from darkness for the prisoners, to proclaim

the year of the Lord's favor and the day of vengeance of our God, to comfort all who mourn, and provide for those who grieve in Zion— to bestow on them a crown of beauty instead of ashes, the oil of joy instead of mourning, and a garment of praise instead of a spirit of despair. They will be called oaks of righteousness, a planting of the Lord for the display of his splendor" (Isaiah 61:1-3 NIV).

SUMMARY OF THE PROCESS

- INTERVENTION: We desperately need God's intervention into our pain, our circumstances, the nitty-gritty of our lives so we can connect with others and love again from our hearts instead of self-protecting our own hearts which is actually the opposite of love.

"Search me, God, and know my heart; test me and know my anxious thoughts. See if there is any offensive way in me, and lead me in the way everlasting" (Psalm 139:23-24 NIV).

- INTEGRATION: Our hearts have become divided, fragmented, broken in pieces just through living in this broken world with others who are also broken. We need to get back our whole heart to be able to love God, ourselves, and others. We need our hearts to be made whole again.

"May God Himself, the God of peace, sanctify you through and through. May your WHOLE spirit, soul and body be kept blameless at the coming of our Lord Jesus Christ" (1 Thessalonians 5:23 NIV).

"The Spirit of the Sovereign LORD is on me, because the LORD has anointed me to proclaim good news to the poor. He has sent me to bind up the BROKEN-HEARTED, to proclaim freedom for the captives and release from darkness for the prisoners" (Isaiah 61:1 NIV).

"Give me an UNDIVIDED HEART..." (Psalm 86:11 NIV).

- INTIMACY: Inviting the Spirit of God to search us deeply in order to give us back our whole hearts from the destruction of the pain. That allows us to experience a new intimacy with our own hearts, with the heart of God, and with others. Are you willing to invite God to introduce you to the true "you" he has always known and loved?

"You have searched me, LORD, and you know me" (Psalm 139:1 NIV).

- INTEGRITY: Integration and intimacy opens the door to our being able to live with a greater level of integrity. Integrity is a fruit that grows from our hearts when the integration of our broken pieces begin to connect again in wholeness. We begin to see double mindedness release it's hold, enabling us to increasingly be able to:

"'Love the Lord your God with ALL YOUR HEART and with ALL YOUR SOUL and with ALL YOUR MIND.' And the second is like it: 'Love your neighbor as yourself'" (Matthew 22:37, 39).

- IDENTITY: We begin to become our real selves, discover and enjoy our true hearts, and become the self God has always known and loved. He is the one who knew us prior to the robbery of this broken and hurtful world and desires to introduce us to ourselves! I've never met a person who didn't discover an amazing love for themselves when they finally met that person who was hiding within.

- IT IS NO LONGER **"I"** WHO LIVES, BUT CHRIST WHO LIVES IN ME: As we get our lives back from the robbery of the pain, we can begin to learn to trust again. It becomes safer to surrender our lives into God's capable hands instead of trying to figure it out all on our own. Life becomes about joining Him on the unique pathways He has created us to walk on with Him. Living each day becomes a co-labor and we are no longer walking alone. We get our lives back from the robbery of the thief (the enemy - John 10:10) so we can lay them down to the "Author" of our lives who truly knows the way into our futures. Life isn't all about *us* anymore, but instead lived with Him who gave up His own life for me.

PART THREE: YOUR YOUNGER SELF

"'I' have been crucified with Christ and I no longer live, but Christ lives in me. The life I now live in the body, I live by faith in the Son of God, who loved me and gave Himself for me" (Galatians 2:3, 20 NIV).

"For I know the plans I have for you," declares the LORD, "plans to prosper you and not to harm you, plans to give you hope and a future" (Jeremiah 29:11 NIV).

CONCLUSION

We all desire to be free and not live any longer with a broken heart. However, just through living in this broken world, we have all been wounded, hurt, used, and too many times, even abused. That cannot be just swept under the rug, but must be faced, and felt, so we can be healed and restored.

The Result:

- You meet Jesus as the Healer as you embrace the pain you experienced
- You feel and name the emotions originally experienced and can finally release them to Him who also suffered those same feelings
- You begin to embrace that little child within you who originally experienced the hurt and you invite Jesus to embrace him/her as well. Remember, Jesus is always knocking, waiting for your invitation.
- You ask the child's forgiveness for locking their pain away, abandoning them, and rejecting that part of ourselves
- You allow Jesus the forgiver (who is not an excuser) to help you release the offender to Him and forgive them from your heart, not just from your mind

"Surely ***He took up our pain and bore our suffering****, yet we considered Him punished by God, stricken by Him, and afflicted.*

But He was pierced for our transgressions, He was crushed for our iniquities; the punishment that brought us peace was on Him, ***and by His wounds we are healed***" (Isaiah 53:4-5 NIV).

"Since the children have flesh and blood, He too shared in their humanity so that by His death He might break the power of him who holds the power of death— that is, the devil— and free those who all their lives were held in slavery by their fear of death" (Hebrews 2:14,15).

There are many so called "deaths" that we can fear that are not just physical deaths.

We may fear a "death" through losses of relationships (divorce, for example), the fear of abandonment, or feeling left all alone.

Some may fear the "death" of money, security and finances through loss of a job or career. These are just a few examples of different "deaths" we may fear.

"For this reason He had to be made like them, fully human in every way, in order that He might become a merciful and faithful high priest in service to God and that He might make atonement for the sins of the people. Because He Himself suffered when He was tempted, He is able to help those who are being tempted" (Hebrews 2:14-15, 17,18 NIV).

CHRIST IN ME THE HOPE OF GLORY

THE KEY TO LIVING OUR TRUE LIVES

"To them God has chosen to make known among the Gentiles the glorious riches of this mystery, which is Christ in you, the hope of glory" (Colossians 1:27 NIV).

Jesus is not far off. He is closer than our breath, ever present with us if we have invited Him to live within us. We then are meant to draw our life from His life inside us. Picture an old- fashioned deep well with a bucket. Drawing from His life is similar to allowing our bucket to be lowered deeply into that well inside us to draw up the water into our pail.

"With joy you will draw water from the wells of salvation" (Isaiah 12:3 NIV).

We cannot live our lives from two centers. We will either live from the shame lies we have believed about ourselves at our core, or we will get out of agreement with them, and live from Christ in us!

We cannot serve two masters.

"I have been crucified with Christ and I no longer live, but Christ lives in me. The life I now live in the body, I live by faith in the Son of God, who loved me and gave Himself for me" (Galatians 2:20 NIV).

When we remain united with Him, flowing together in unity and harmony with His purposes instead of our own, life becomes so much easier. We just show up for life, whatever our lives are meant to look like on that particular day. His yoke is easy, and His burden is truly light.

"Come to me, all you who are weary and burdened, and I will give you rest. Take my yoke upon you and learn from me, for I am gentle and humble in heart, and you will find rest for your souls. For my yoke is easy and my burden is light" (Matthew 11:28-30 NIV).

When we are willing to do things with Him instead of for Him, and live our lives God's way instead of our way, He gives us the grace and strength to walk into that which He calls us to.

The problems arise when we begin to do things our own way, and when we determine what is "good" instead of allowing Him to work out all things to the good.

"And we know that in all things God works for the good of those who love Him, who have been called according to his purpose" (Romans 8:28 NIV).

We begin to recognize doing our own "good" might cause us to do good things, but not necessarily the things we are created for that He is calling us to do. We often find ourselves weary and eventually burned out by doing "good things" for the Lord.

Jesus only did what he saw his Father doing. He allowed his Father to determine what was good.

"For we are His workmanship, created in Christ Jesus for good works, which God prepared beforehand so that we would walk in them" (Ephesians 2:10 NASB).

We are meant to live our lives by co-laboring with Christ in us. We cannot do true life without Him.

"Remain in me, as I also remain in you. No branch can bear fruit by itself; it must remain in the vine. Neither can you bear fruit unless you remain in me. "I am the vine; you are the branches. If you remain in me and I in you, you will bear much fruit; apart from me you can do nothing" (John 15:4-5 NIV).

We can obviously do many things on our own, but only the things done with Him have true value and that value remains for all eternity!

As we become more and more surrendered to Him and His ways, we become more sensitive to the "checks" He puts within our spirits, and we become increasingly aware as to when to stop moving forward. We learn to wait and listen. We begin to learn to walk in tune with His Spirit and that creates a grace and peace within us as we move forward. Then when a "check" comes, we stop. Too many times we don't know exactly what He is doing in any given situation so we must NOT lean on our own understanding or interpretation.

"Trust in the Lord with all your heart and lean not on your own understanding; in all your ways submit to Him, and He will make your paths straight" (Proverbs 3:5,6 NIV).

Living our authentic life only becomes possible when we walk out our lives from the inside out with Him. We don't know the way of real life, but Jesus does because He is that life. He will lead us and guide us into truth because He is the only absolute truth. Jesus says, *"I am the way and the truth and the life"* (John 14:6 NIV).

"'For My thoughts are not your thoughts, neither are your ways My ways,' declares the Lord. 'As the heavens are higher than the earth, so are My ways higher than your ways and My thoughts than your thoughts'" (Isaiah 55:8,9 NIV).

Our true lives are not just about us. We have been chosen and called to co-labor with Him for larger purposes than we could ever have imagined. The smaller stories we are currently living are meant to fit into an eternal larger story that He is unfolding on planet earth. We each have a part of it, a sphere of influence that He is weaving together with His eternal purposes. However we can only fulfill those purposes *with* Him and not *for* Him.

We are limited in what we can even see or understand so we must rely on, trust in, lean on the Spirit of Jesus to walk with us. We are truly clueless because only He is real life Himself who chooses to dwell within us and include us in the eternal larger story He is writing on planet earth! *"For in Him we live and move and have our being"* (Acts 17:28 NIV).

"For from Him and through Him and for Him are all things. To Him be the glory forever! Amen" (Romans 11:36 NIV).

Made in the USA
Columbia, SC
28 January 2020

87222754R00055